FLOWMAN AND THE MAGIC MULLET

**STORY BY
KONN & EMILY HAWKES
ILLUSTRATIONS BY EMILY HAWKES**

Copyright © 2021 Emily Hawkes.
First Edition May 2021.

All rights reserved, including the right to reproduce this book or portions thereof in any form whatsoever. Apart from any fair dealing for the purpose of research, private study, criticism or review, no part of this publication may be reproduced, stored in, or introduced into a retrieval system, or transmitted in any form or by any means (electronic, mechanical, photocopying, recording or otherwise), without the prior written permission of the copyright owner.

FLOWMAN AND THE MAGIC MULLET by Konn & Emily Hawkes
Illustrations by Emily Hawkes
ISBN: 978-1-7776417-0-2 Paperback
ISBN: 978-1-7776417-1-9 Ebook

HockeyHair logo provided by HockeyHair LLC
www.hockeyhairco.com
Reprinted with permission.

There is a kid who loves hockey more than life itself.
Scoring point after point - always shooting top shelf.
He moves on the ice like a cheetah on skates.
His slap shot is feared by both foes and teammates.

In the city of Calgary he is Captain of his team.
He's got a sweet mullet and he is livin' the dream.
His lettuce is fresh and the ladies they all stare.
His name is Greg Flowman...they call him, "The Hair."

Everybody loves Greg's hair, except for his mom.
Ms. Flowman does not like his mullet - she says it's too long.
She's tried to cut Greg's hair countless times in the past.
He always runs away. That kid is shifty, and he's fast.
"You can't cut my flow! The boys will chirp and they'll beak.
Mom, without my sick mullet my game will be weak.
The girls love my hair and the guys all do too.
Like Brad, Peach, Reno, and Great-Uncle Hugh!"

One night before bed, Flowman lathered his locks,
with mousse and gel and other products.
He looked in the mirror and said, "What a fox!
My hair is so rad. It's awesome. It rocks!"

The next morning when he awoke, he ran his fingers through his hair.
To Flowman's shock and dismay his sweet locks were not there.
"This is unreal! What's happened to me?
My mullet is gone! This can't possibly be!"

Flowman knew right away his mom was to blame.
"Mom, what have you done? You've just ruined my game!
I'm Greg 'The Hair' Flowman! Now, what will they call me?
My sweet loaf is gone. I'm a bald hairless phoney!"
Flowman's mom began to giggle as she shook her head.
She shared some words of wisdom and here is what she said.
"It's all in your mind, Greg. Your game will be fine.
You still have your shot. You've played hundreds of times.
I believe in you, son. You've got what it takes.
Just play with your heart, and you'll make no mistakes.
It's not about winning but trying your best.
So just give it your all; put your skills to the test."

Flowman raced to the garage and grabbed his gear.
He shot pucks at the wall as he watched in the mirror.
He wound up and took a shot, but he missed the puck.
"Oh my gosh, what's happened? I'm terrible - bad luck!
Mom, you've ruined my game. I'll never score another goal!
My mullet was lucky. It had heart. It had soul."

The loss of Flowman's hair was really quite tragic,
and he began to believe that his mullet was magic!
It was this very moment, he said to himself,
"My hair is my strength . . . my ticket to wealth.
From this day forward, it is this I declare . . .
my flow will fly free for my name is 'The Hair!' "

Flowman knew there was only one thing left to do.
He refused to cut his hair . . . so it grew, and it grew . . .

And it grew . . .

And it grew . . .

And it grew . . .

By the age of twenty, he was rolling in dough.
Flowman even found companies to sponsor his flow.
But one day his magic mullet nearly cost him his career;
and it happened at the most important game of the year.

For what was about to happen, he could not prepare.
An unthinkable moment for Greg 'The Hair.'
His team was ahead by a single goal.
With two minutes left, it was a sight to behold.

Flowman skated down the ice with the puck on his stick.
His speed was supersonic; his skills were so sick.
Then suddenly, his mullet got caught in his skates,
and he tripped and crashed into his own teammates.

The skate blades were so sharp that they cut Flowman's hair. His magic mullet was gone! What a dreadful nightmare!

The other team skated by and shot a slapper through the air.
It landed in the net with just seconds to spare.

Flowman was in shock, his precious hair was no more.
Without his magic mullet his game would be poor.
The coach called a time-out and Flowman raced off the ice.
"If you put me back in, Coach, you'll all pay the price!"
"That's nonsense!" Coach yelled as he ran through the play.
"You'll drag then you'll dangle, this way, then that way.
Don't give up, Flowman, we're counting on you!
Now get back on the ice and just do what you do!"

'The Hair' took a deep breath and looked up in the stands,
and there sat his mom . . . Flowman's number one fan.
He began to remember the wise words she once said.
He could hear her words echo inside of his head.
"I believe in you, son. You've got what it takes.
Just play with your heart, and you'll make no mistakes."

At that second Flowman realized his hair wasn't magic.
His success was because of mad skills and sick hat tricks.
His confidence grew with each passing moment,
so he skated to center ice to face his opponents.
With a smile on his face, Flowman knew what to do.
The referee dropped the puck as the whistle blew.

Flowman won the face-off and skated with might.
The fans rose to their feet in spectacular delight.
As he rushed to the goal line with seconds on the clock,
he toe dragged, he dangled and then shot the puck.

WOO WOO WOO WOO!!!! The siren blared.
Flowman scored the winning goal, and he didn't need his hair.

As for Flowman's magic mullet . . . well, it had no superpowers, you see.
The true magic was within himself, always longing to be free.
Make no mistake, Flowman loved his hair and certainly always would.
But now he does not need his mullet to know his game is good.

As the years passed by, Flowman's locks grew into a shiny new mullet.
By the time he was forty years old, it had turned into a skullet.
Though no matter how hairless, how bald, or how bare,
Greg Flowman would forever be known as 'The Hair.'

About the Authors

Konn Hawkes hails from Watrous, Saskatchewan. It was in this small town where Konn grew up and developed a love and respect for the game of hockey. After years of perfecting his toe drags and dangles, he went on to play for the Melfort Mustangs of the SJHL. Konn's hard work and dedication paid off, and he was fortunate to receive a Division 1 hockey scholarship to Sacred Heart University in Fairfield, Connecticut. It was at Sacred Heart where he met his wife and best friend, Emily. When Konn isn't scoring a backhand shelf in the local rec hockey league, you'll find him tending to his crops on his family farm where they grow a variety of wheat, lentils, barley, and canola.

Emily Hawkes is originally from the town of Walpole, New Hampshire. From the time Emily could pick up a crayon she always had a love for drawing. When she was eight years old, her parents gifted her private art lessons for her birthday. Her art teacher later told Emily's parents that she would no longer provide these lessons because all Emily wanted to do was to draw cartoons, and she was a serious artist and didn't have time for such childish nonsense. Fast forward 30 years later, Emily has written and illustrated her very first children's book, *Flowman & the Magic Mullet*. Emily currently lives in Watrous, Saskatchewan with her husband, Konn. In addition to being a huge hockey fan (LET'S GO, CAPS!), Emily spends her time helping out on the farm and tending to her honeybee apiary with her dog Bo always by her side.

Made in United States
North Haven, CT
18 September 2023